52
Weeks to Owning Who You Are

THE
CHALLENGE
TO
CHANGE

ELDRIDGE BROUSSARD

BROUSSARD **BE** ENTERPRISES

BE INSPIRED · BE ENCOURAGED · BE COURAGEOUS ·

The Challenge to Change

Published by Broussard Enterprises

ISBN 978-0-9909531-2-8

CONTENTS

INTRODUCTION

A lot of "quote books" feature snappy remarks from famous people that make us smile or laugh, raise an eyebrow or get emotional—but the quotation doesn't do much for us, other than spark a quick reaction. We snicker or tear up, and then put down the book and go about our business as usual.

This isn't one of those quote books.

I developed this simple resource to help leaders facilitate the process of personal growth, whether individually or in group settings. Each of the fifty-two quotations I have highlighted has played an important role in my own development, and I believe that by examining them throughout the year, one each week, you will find yourself inspired, encouraged, and also challenged.

As potent as the quotations are, however, the most important part of this resource is the work you will do yourself in the "Making It Work for You" sections. Over the next twelve months, I'll ask you to focus on one quotation per week. To help you interact with the ideas behind the quotations, I'll ask you to respond to five different questions, one per day, from Monday through Friday. In these times of personal exploration, I expect that you'll find some crucial answers for yourself about who you are and what you're on this earth to accomplish.

In other words, I've designed this little book as a guide to help you *Own Who You Are.* By the end of the year, when you look back over what you've written in the workbook (and separate journal), I hope you'll have created a working plan to be very intentional about how you influence yourself and the people who choose to follow you.

As you spend some quality time interacting with this brief resource over the next year, I'm convinced it will make a significant impact on your life, in your classroom, and in your home.

Thanks for joining me on the journey!

Eldridge J. Broussard III

GO YOU!

It's a new week and a new month. If you haven't been rooting for yourself lately now is the time to begin! Be your biggest supporter, biggest cheerleader. Encourage, enlighten, empower yourself. Vow to never let yourself down. Change your thinking, get busy working toward the positive and be transformed.

CHALENE JOHNSON

"Before you can inspire with emotion, you must be swamped with it yourself. Before you can move their tears, your own must flow. To convince them, you must yourself believe."

 What inspires you the most about life?

 What emotions do you tend to feel most strongly?

 When do you feel most moved emotionally?

 Describe the last time you had an emotional outburst. What triggered it? What emotions were wrapped up in that experience?

 Name the top values or beliefs that guide your life.

WEEK **2**

"Our greatest enemies, the ones we must fight most often, are within."

UNKNOWN

MONDAY What external forces do you face that you consider "enemies"?

TUESDAY How do you generally deal with conflict?

WEDNESDAY What regular practices of yours tend to harm your health and wellness?

THURSDAY What internal fights have you struggled with over the last several months?

FRIDAY What internal fights do you need to gear up for? How can you best prepare to win in those areas of life?

WEEK 3

"At every crisis in one's life, it is absolute salvation to have some sympathetic friend to whom you can think aloud without restraint or misgiving."

PRESIDENT WOODROW WILSON

MONDAY

Think of the worst time in your life. Who was there for you?

TUESDAY

When you are in need, what do you lose if you have no shoulder to lean on? What prevents you from seeking out that shoulder?

WEDNESDAY

What keeps you from asking for help when you are in crisis?

THURSDAY

Suppose you want to share from the heart with another person, but you hesitate. What stops you exposing what's on your heart?

FRIDAY

How can you become more of a safe haven for those around you in their time of need?

WEEK 4

"If you have nothing to lose, you've already lost!"

ELDRIDGE J. BROUSSARD III

MONDAY What are you most grateful for in life?

TUESDAY How does hopelessness steal your passion and value as a person?

WEDNESDAY What would the world lose if it lost you?

THURSDAY What things in life would you be willing to fight for? Is there anything in life for which you'd be willing to die?

FRIDAY How can you keep your passion alive when you feel discouraged?

WEEK **5**

"The number one reason why people give up so fast is because they tend to look at how far they still have to go, instead of how far they have gotten."

UNKNOWN

MONDAY

What factors make it easy for you to throw in the towel and give up?

TUESDAY

What are your top excuses for not moving forward and growing where you know you should?

WEDNESDAY

How close are you to achieving your key goals in life? Put a percentage to it.

THURSDAY

Describe a time when you were able to push through and persevere. What feelings attach to that memory?

FRIDAY

What will it cost you to stay where you are and make no progress?

WEEK **6**

"Fear has two meanings:
     Forget
     Everything
     And
     Run
or
     Face
     Everything
     And
     Rise.
The choice is yours."

UNKNOWN

MONDAY How does fear in your life affect your self-image?

TUESDAY Do you think you are truly able to forget your fears? Why or why not?

WEDNESDAY What specific fears cause you to run?

THURSDAY What risks come with facing your fears?

FRIDAY What would life look like if you could rise above your fear?

WEEK **7**

"There is only
one way to
avoid criticism:
do nothing,
say nothing,
and be nothing."

ARISTOTLE

MONDAY

Suppose someone needed to offer you some critique. How could the person most effectively approach you?

TUESDAY

Why does it often feel safer to "do nothing" than to "do something"?

WEDNESDAY

How do you feel, physically or emotionally, when someone criticizes you?

THURSDAY

How could you learn from your critics, instead of letting their critiques paralyze you?

FRIDAY

Describe the people in your life who offer the greatest encouragement to you. Let them know this week what their encouragement means to you.

WEEK **8**

"Anger is an acid that can do more harm to the vessel in which it is stored than to anything on which it is poured."

MARK TWAIN

MONDAY

How could anger stunt your growth and steal your ability to enjoy life?

TUESDAY

How do you think anger and forgiveness might be connected in your life?

WEDNESDAY

How has resentment kept you from moving forward?

THURSDAY

What is preventing you from releasing the anger you feel? What will you do to release that anger?

FRIDAY

What would it feel like to live without anger and resentment? Describe what it might look like if you lived free from unforgiveness.

"Learn to give your absence to those who don't appreciate your presence."

MONDAY

Who in your life truly shows appreciation for you?

TUESDAY

What role does gratitude play in your life?

WEDNESDAY

What are some possible signs that you're not being valued?

THURSDAY

Is there anyone from whom you might need to distance yourself? Explain.

FRIDAY

What values do you bring to your relationships?

"Lord,
I am thankful
that I don't look
like what I've
been through."

UNKNOWN

MONDAY

What emotional or physical scars do you carry? From where do they come?

TUESDAY

What parts of your past have you dealt with successfully, and what parts are still affecting your future in a negative way?

WEDNESDAY

Has a trial you've faced ever turned into something beautiful? Describe how something productive came from something challenging.

THURSDAY

When you look in the mirror, what do you see that makes you feel proud?

FRIDAY

How do you let your outer appearance reflect your inner self?

WEEK **11**

"The past cannot be changed, forgotten, edited or erased; it can only be embraced."

UNKNOWN

MONDAY

What circumstances of your past do you need to accept?

TUESDAY

How much time have you spent trying to change or erase your past? Were you successful in this endeavor? Why or why not?

WEDNESDAY

What are some possible benefits of not being able to forget your past—even the challenges and mistakes?

THURSDAY

How can you reconcile with others for the mistakes you have made? List those people to whom you need to apologize.

FRIDAY

If you were going to fully accept your past, what would the process look like? What tools, resources and support would you need?

'Finished last' will always be better than 'did not finish,' which always trumps 'did not start.'

UNKNOWN

MONDAY

Describe a time where you did not win but you still were able to finish. What did it feel like to finish?

TUESDAY

What is the greater accomplishment: To participate, to finish, or to win? Explain your reasoning.

WEDNESDAY

What keeps you from starting the things you want to accomplish?

THURSDAY

What barriers do you face when trying to complete difficult tasks?

FRIDAY

What tasks or dreams would be most important for you to complete if you knew you had only a year to live?

"It's not selfish to love yourself, take care of yourself, and to make your happiness a priority. It's a necessity."

MONDAY

Define love in your own words. Do you truly love yourself, according to your definition?

TUESDAY

Think about the person you love most in the world. How would your life change if you treated yourself as you treat the person you love the most?

WEDNESDAY

How can you balance loving yourself and caring for others? What elements are required for each?

THURSDAY

What habits of self-care can you implement this week to love yourself better?

FRIDAY

How can you see taking care of yourself as an investment in your ability to love others well?

WEEK **14**

"Dear past:
'Thanks for all
the lessons.'

Dear future:
'I'm ready.'"

MONDAY — Name the greatest lesson you have learned in life.

TUESDAY — Describe the legacy you would like to leave for your loved ones?

WEDNESDAY — What would need to change for you to feel completely ready to embrace your future?

THURSDAY — How can you let the past teach you, instead of hold you back?

FRIDAY — Write a simple motto that will help you live in the moment each day. What does your motto mean to you?

"People will
love you, people
will hate you
and none of
it will have
anything to
do with you."

ABRAHAM HICKS

MONDAY

What do people love most about you? What do you love most about yourself?

TUESDAY

How does the opinion of others affect your outlook on your life?

WEDNESDAY

What would it be like to balance the expectations others have of you with the expectations you have of yourself? What would it look like within your current circumstances?

THURSDAY

How have you allowed your identity to get wrapped up in the opinions of others?

FRIDAY

Who have you judged because of your own biases? Do you think your bias had more to do with the particular person or with the lens through which you see yourself and the world?

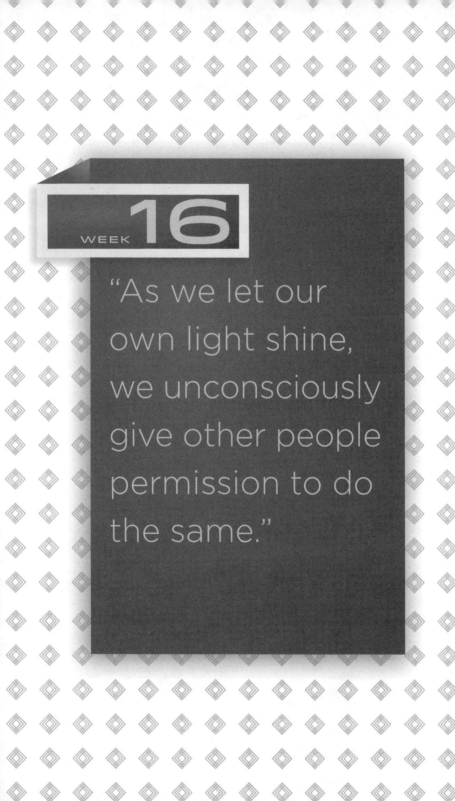

WEEK **16**

"As we let our own light shine, we unconsciously give other people permission to do the same."

MONDAY

What would it mean for you to have your light shine?

TUESDAY

Who in your life has given you permission to shine? How can you show them your appreciation?

WEDNESDAY

What are you intentionally giving to others as a result of who you are?

THURSDAY

Why is understanding who you are critical to your ability to influence others?

FRIDAY

What permission do you need to give yourself that will foster your personal growth?

WEEK 17

"You've been criticizing your-self for years and it hasn't worked; try approving of yourself and see what happens."

 **MONDAY** Describe some times when you have harshly criticized yourself? What prompted that criticism?

 **TUESDAY** What role does negative self-talk play in your lack of personal growth?

 WEDNESDAY What would it look like to give yourself constructive criticism?

THURSDAY Does the thought of offering yourself approval and acceptance cause you any anxiety? If so, what about this scares you?

FRIDAY What might change in your life if you looked at possible solutions to your challenges, instead of focusing primarily on the problem?

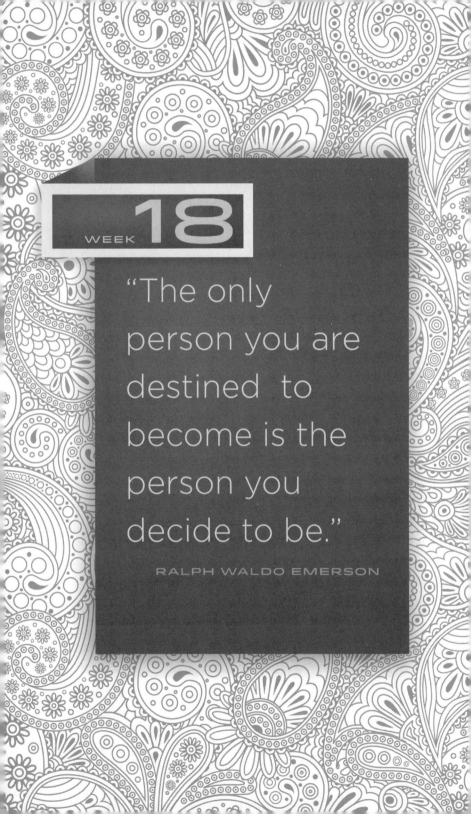

WEEK **18**

"The only person you are destined to become is the person you decide to be."

RALPH WALDO EMERSON

MONDAY

What do you believe about destiny and fate?

TUESDAY

When you were a child, how did you envision your adult life? In what ways has your mental picture come true? In what ways has it missed the mark?

WEDNESDAY

How do you think circumstances have shaped who you have become?

THURSDAY

Describe the person you would like to be in the future. What will you need to change to become that person?

FRIDAY

Who will you decide to be from this point forward?

WEEK **19**

"Fear and Faith have something in common. They both ask us to BELIEVE in something we cannot see."

JOEL OSTEEN

MONDAY How does fear affect your life?

TUESDAY What does it look like to really live your faith?

WEDNESDAY Why is what you believe so critical to who you are as a person?

THURSDAY How have you allowed fear to manifest itself in your relationships and goals?

FRIDAY What would it take for you to allow faith to conquer your fear? What challenges come up for you as you ponder this question?

WEEK **20**

"A vision is not just a picture of what could be— it is an appeal to our better selves, a call to become something more."

ROSABETH MOSS KANTER

MONDAY Describe your vision for your life.

TUESDAY What about your vision seems unattainable or far-fetched?

WEDNESDAY Describe what you see as your "best self."

THURSDAY How can you keep from stumbling into "doing more" versus "being more"?

FRIDAY How would you describe the benefits of fulfilling your vision? How would you convince yourself of the importance of working hard to make your vision a reality?

WEEK 21

"Don't be a victim of negative self-talk. Remember, you are listening."

BOB PROCTOR

MONDAY

Name the top triggers that tend to send you spiraling into negative self-talk.

TUESDAY

How can you silence negative voices and replace them with positive ones?

WEDNESDAY

In what ways have you made yourself a "victim" of your own brutality?

THURSDAY

What role do you think your "thought life" plays into your actions and behaviors?

FRIDAY

Who can be a positive voice in your life when you can't seem to shake the negative ones?

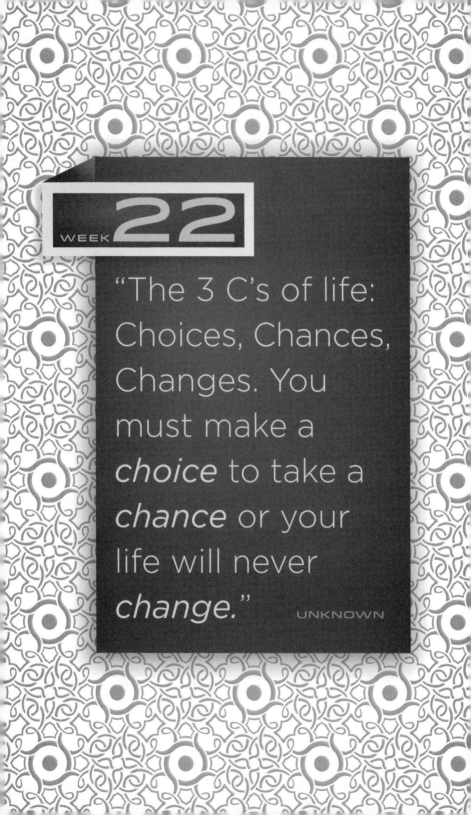

WEEK **22**

"The 3 C's of life: Choices, Chances, Changes. You must make a *choice* to take a *chance* or your life will never *change.*" UNKNOWN

MONDAY

How have the choices you have made positively affected your life and the lives of others? How have your choices negatively impacted those same people?

TUESDAY

Do you choose to see life in a mostly positive or mostly negative manner? Why do you think you see things this way?

WEDNESDAY

Describe some times when you took full advantage of the chances and opportunities afforded you. What chances and opportunities have you missed?

THURSDAY

Describe your thoughts, feelings and attitudes toward change.

FRIDAY

How do you negotiate reasonable risks in your life, especially when faced with the challenge of making a significant change?

"The best years of your life are the ones in which you decide your problems are your own."

UNKNOWN

MONDAY

What do you think of when you imagine the "best years of your life"?

TUESDAY

How do you know when a burden is too heavy to bear on your own?

WEDNESDAY

What barriers have you found that keep you from taking full responsibility for your actions, choices and problems?

THURSDAY

How do you "own" your problems without "going it alone"?

FRIDAY

How do the concepts of "freedom" and "responsibility" interact in your mind?

WEEK **24**

"To genuinely invest in people you have to be genuinely interested in them."

UNKNOWN

MONDAY

Who has made an important investment in your life? What did he or she do?

TUESDAY

What ways, other than money, can you invest in another person?

WEDNESDAY

How do you differentiate between someone who has your best interest in mind versus someone who has selfish motives?

THURSDAY

How do you like others to show their interest in you?

FRIDAY

Name some people you can connect with this week on a genuine and intentional level. How can you show your interest and engagement in their lives and in their journey?

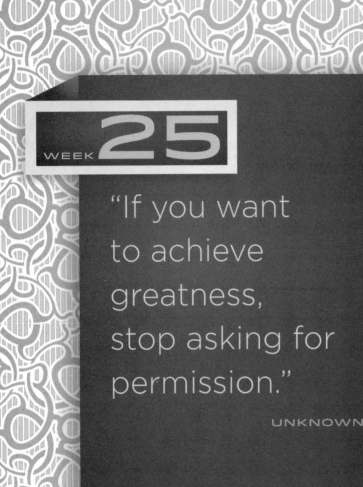

WEEK 25

"If you want
to achieve
greatness,
stop asking for
permission."

UNKNOWN

MONDAY

What does greatness look like for you?

TUESDAY

What would you say are the steps to achieving success?

WEDNESDAY

What holds you back from achieving your own definition of success? Describe your plan for achieving that success.

THURSDAY

Why does asking for permission from others make it harder for you to achieve greatness?

FRIDAY

What permissions do you need to give yourself to enable you to grow without false limits?

"Having the answers is not essential to living. What is essential is knowing there is an answer and being determined to find it."

UNKNOWN

MONDAY

What would your life be like if you had "all the answers"?

TUESDAY

What questions are most essential for you to ask in order to find the answers you need?

WEDNESDAY

What would change if you focused on the journey instead of where you hope to ultimately end up?

THURSDAY

What answers do you need to find within yourself?

FRIDAY

What is holding you back from looking for the answers you need?

"I am not a
product of my
circumstances.
I am a product
of my decisions."

UNKNOWN

MONDAY

How have your circumstances helped to shape you?

TUESDAY

What role does "choice" play in your understanding of dealing with difficult personal circumstances?

WEDNESDAY

What good decisions have you made in the midst of difficult circumstances?

THURSDAY

Describe your game plan for overcoming a difficult environment.

FRIDAY

What holds you back from fully embracing the power of choice? What will you do differently, moving forward?

"You can't move forward if you stay chained to the past."

UNKNOWN

MONDAY

In what area(s) of your life do you want to grow? In what area(s) of your life do you need to grow?

TUESDAY

What factors stop you from moving forward?

WEDNESDAY

What unhelpful patterns of your past have become too comfortable? How will you change those patterns?

THURSDAY

Think about the past as a series of links on a chain. Describe the links that are holding you back.

FRIDAY

What is your plan to remove each hurtful link so that you can grow?

WEEK 29

"Never make permanent decisions on the basis of temporary emotions."

UNKNOWN

MONDAY

How often do you allow emotions to control your choices?

TUESDAY

List the major choices you are facing now. Which choices bring up the most powerful emotions for you?

WEDNESDAY

Which permanent decisions have you made in the past that you now wish you could change? What were you feeling at the time you made each of those choices?

THURSDAY

What emotion do you feel most strongly when you have a big decision to make? Why do you think that particular emotion tends to surface?

FRIDAY

What steps will you take to remember to pause and process your emotions before you make big decisions? Who will help you to process you choices and your emotions?

"Speak in such away that others love to listen to you. Listen in such a way that others love to speak to you."

UNKNOWN

MONDAY

Who in your life do you love listening to? What is it about that person that makes the experience so uplifting? What will you do to emulate this person in the way you speak?

TUESDAY

How were you spoken to as a child? How might that personal history influence how you speak to others today?

WEDNESDAY

What negative habits would you like to change about the way you communicate? How will you make those changes?

THURSDAY

Describe what it feels like to be truly heard by someone who deeply cares for you.

FRIDAY

Think about the people in your life who don't especially like listening to you. How will you speak differently to them so they might hear you better?

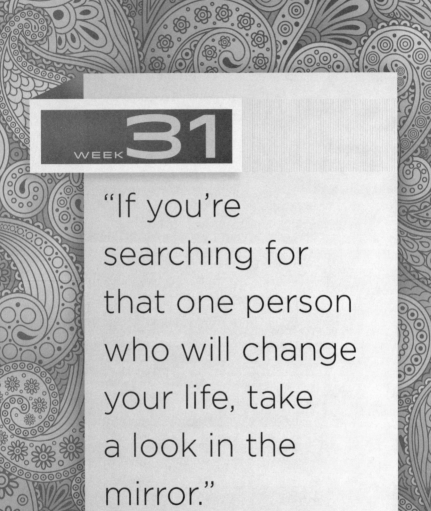

WEEK **31**

"If you're searching for that one person who will change your life, take a look in the mirror."

UNKNOWN

MONDAY

What about your life do you most want to change? How will you start making those changes?

TUESDAY

How are your daily choices keeping you stuck?

WEDNESDAY

What would happen if you took control of everything for which you are responsible, and released everything you cannot control?

THURSDAY

What skills, talents and experiences do you have that uniquely equip you to carry your own load?

FRIDAY

Spend some time looking in the mirror. What do you see that you love? What do you see that you want to change? What are the important things about you that cannot be seen in a mirror?

"Success is liking yourself, liking what you do, and liking how you do it."

MAYA ANGELOU

MONDAY

How have you allowed others to define "success" in your life? How will this change, moving forward?

TUESDAY

What is standing in the way of you truly liking and accepting yourself?

WEDNESDAY

If you could do anything with the rest of your life, what would you do? Why did you choose this?

THURSDAY

What is your personal definition of success? How did you arrive at this definition?

FRIDAY

How do you think you would feel if you were completely successful, by your own definition? What would it take to achieve that kind of success?

"Forgiveness is making a conscious decision to live in the present even if the past still hurts."

UNKNOWN

MONDAY

What scares you the most about forgiveness?

TUESDAY

How well is holding onto the past serving you in the present?

WEDNESDAY

What would living fully in the moment look like for you?

THURSDAY

What parts of the past can you choose to forgive, even if you cannot forget?

FRIDAY

How can you use the hurts of your past to prompt you to grow in a healthy way?

"You should always be learning. If you're the smartest person in the room, you're in the wrong place."

UNKNOWN

MONDAY

What does it mean to be a "lifelong learner"? How will you become a lifelong learner?

TUESDAY

What are you learning right now through your life experiences, especially the difficult and challenging ones?

WEDNESDAY

Describe the difference between being "wise" and being "smart." Which of the two qualities would you rather possess? Why?

THURSDAY

Who are the people around you who challenge you and sharpen you?

FRIDAY

Practice being a "student" of others the next time you are in a group. Listen more than you speak and try to learn something new. What is difficult for you about this challenge?

"If it doesn't challenge you, it won't change you."

UNKNOWN

MONDAY Describe the biggest challenge you have ever faced.

TUESDAY What have you overcome in your life that has changed you for the better?

WEDNESDAY Why is being challenged difficult and even painful at times?

THURSDAY What challenges do you need to give yourself so you will take action in ways that will help you to grow and change?

FRIDAY Write about your current challenges. How will you be intentional about being thankful for these challenges?

WEEK **36**

"It hurts because it's real. It hurts because it mattered. And that's an important thing to acknowledge to yourself."

UNKNOWN

MONDAY

Which hurts in your life have you tried to suppress and deny? Why did you respond in this way?

TUESDAY

What might happen if you admitted that your hurts mattered and deserved to be acknowledged?

WEDNESDAY

How has suppressing your hurt allowed you to cope? In the long run, do you feel that this is a healthy option for growth? Why or why not?

THURSDAY

What hurts can you decide to release right now by admitting they were real and they mattered?

FRIDAY

The next time you suffer a deep hurt, what can you do to make sure you process the pain in a healthy manner?

WEEK **37**

"You teach
people how to
treat you by
what you allow,
what you stop
and what you
reinforce."

TONY GASKINS

MONDAY

How have you allowed people to treat you, whether by your action or inaction?

TUESDAY

What boundaries do you need to set for yourself and others regarding the treatment you want to receive?

WEDNESDAY

Think of the person who treats you the worst. How have you allowed this behavior to continue, either with your action or inaction?

THURSDAY

What things do you need to stop allowing in your life? What will be difficult about this process?

FRIDAY

How does your self-talk reinforce how you treat yourself, whether for good or ill? How does your self-talk need to change so that you stop treating yourself poorly?

"Once you've accepted your flaws, no one can use them against you."

UNKNOWN

MONDAY

What do you consider your biggest physical flaws and imperfections? How does it feel to write down the things you don't like about your body?

TUESDAY

Which of your personality traits and character qualities do you wish were different? Why?

WEDNESDAY

Describe true self-acceptance. Do you think you can ever reach a place where you accept yourself fully, flaws and all? Explain.

THURSDAY

How have your flaws added strength to your character?

FRIDAY

What would you need to do to see your flaws as assets and indicators of needed growth?

WEEK **39**

"You were born to make mistakes, not to fake perfection."

UNKNOWN

MONDAY

What scares you about making mistakes?

TUESDAY

How honest are you with yourself about your imperfections and mistakes? How honest are you about these things with others?

WEDNESDAY

What "masks" have you been putting on to fit in?

THURSDAY

What do you believe "perfection" looks like? Is perfection attainable, in your opinion?
Explain your answer.

FRIDAY

Name the people in your life who accept you unconditionally. These men and women love you, regardless of your mistakes. Why do you think they love you in this way?

"You can't upload love, you can't download time, you can't Google all of life's answers. You must actually live some of your life."

UNKNOWN

MONDAY How has technology negatively affected your relationships?

TUESDAY What benefits can you get from building in-person relationships that you can't get from cyber relationships?

WEDNESDAY How is the image you portray to the world different from your true identity?

THURSDAY What electronics do you want to put down completely? Which ones do you want to put down more frequently? What relationships and hobbies do you want to pick up?

FRIDAY What boundaries will you set to keep you connected and engaged in your life?

WEEK **41**

"People will hate you, rate you, shake you, and break you. But how strong you stand is what makes you."

UNKNOWN

MONDAY

How important to you is the approval of others? Explain your answer.

TUESDAY

How much of your life have you dedicated to people-pleasing? How has that approach worked out for you?

WEDNESDAY

What can you do to deflect or transform the negativity of others?

THURSDAY

What barriers keep you from standing strong against the unpleasant opinions or actions of others?

FRIDAY

What role have you allowed negative people to play in shaping your identity? What factors would you like to shape your identity from now on?

WEEK **42**

"Don't let someone's compliments get to your head, and don't let their criticisms get to your heart."

UNKNOWN

MONDAY

Describe the greatest compliment you ever received. Why was it so meaningful to you?

TUESDAY

Who in your life do you trust to give you genuine compliments?

WEDNESDAY

What people in your life do you trust to give you helpful critique? Are these the same people you trust to compliment you?

THURSDAY

Why is it important to let compliments and criticisms inform you but not define you?

FRIDAY

How can you process compliments in your heart but process criticism in your head? Describe what you would need to do.

WEEK **43**

"At first they'll ask you why you're doing it, but later they'll ask you how you did it."

UNKNOWN

MONDAY

What is the greatest "why" in your life?

TUESDAY

Why is it critical for you to know your purpose before you pursue making a plan?

WEDNESDAY

How do you combat the critique of others when they don't understand your desires or plan?

THURSDAY

Who in your life can help you to develop the "why" behind your passions? Who can help you develop the "how" or the path to reach your goal?

FRIDAY

How can you insure that your plans for success are centered on personal growth and not just proving others wrong?

"Until you value yourself, you will not value your time. Until you value your time, you will not do anything with it."

M. SCOTT PECK

MONDAY

What do you value most about yourself?

TUESDAY

What do the people who love you value most about you? (Don't be afraid to ask them!)

WEDNESDAY

What is your time worth to you? How do you prioritize your time around your many tasks and responsibilities?

THURSDAY

How do you respect the limited time you have? How do you respect and honor the time of others?

FRIDAY

If you truly valued yourself and your time, what in your daily behavior would change? Would you say "yes" to different things? Explain.

"Take pride in how far you have come and have faith in how far you can go."

UNKNOWN

MONDAY

Write down the obstacles you have overcome to get where you are right now. Which obstacles were the most difficult to overcome?

TUESDAY

Who in your life can help you to celebrate your accomplishments and growth? How will you ask them to help you focus on how far you have come?

WEDNESDAY

Why is it difficult to see your own accomplishments and successes?

THURSDAY

What is the role of faith in your understanding of your future?

FRIDAY

How will you plan to celebrate your past, live in the moment, and hope in your future?

"Never give up on a dream just because of the time it will take to accomplish it. The time will pass anyway."

UNKNOWN

 What dreams have you put on hold because of the time investment they require?

 Write down your top three life dreams. If you focused only on accomplishing those goals, how long do you think it would take for them to come to fruition?

 What dreams have others shared with you? How can you encourage them to pursue their dreams?

 What is it costing you to postpone your dreams and plans?

 How can you purpose to be more intentional with your time so that you can consistently work on your goals instead of putting them off?

WEEK **47**

"Somewhere, someone is looking for exactly what you have to offer."

UNKNOWN

MONDAY

What do you uniquely have to offer the world that nobody else can duplicate?

TUESDAY

What do you believe about your innate value as human being?

WEDNESDAY

If you were to create a resume of your character traits and beliefs, what would you include?

THURSDAY

What do you value most in other people? Where do you think these values come from?

FRIDAY

How do you know when someone values you for who you are as opposed to what you can do for him or her? Do you value others for who they are, or do you focus more on what they can do for you?
Explain.

"The only difference between stumbling blocks and stepping stones is the way in which we choose to see and use them."

UNKNOWN

MONDAY

What stumbling blocks have you put in your own way in regard to achieving your goals?

TUESDAY

How can you change your own stumbling blocks into stepping stones?

WEDNESDAY

What is your biggest struggle right now? How can you reframe this struggle to see it as a catalyst for change?

THURSDAY

Who can you turn to when you need help in seeing hope for your situation?

FRIDAY

Sometimes stumbling blocks can seem like walls. How can you break down the walls of your challenges and use them to create a path to your healing?

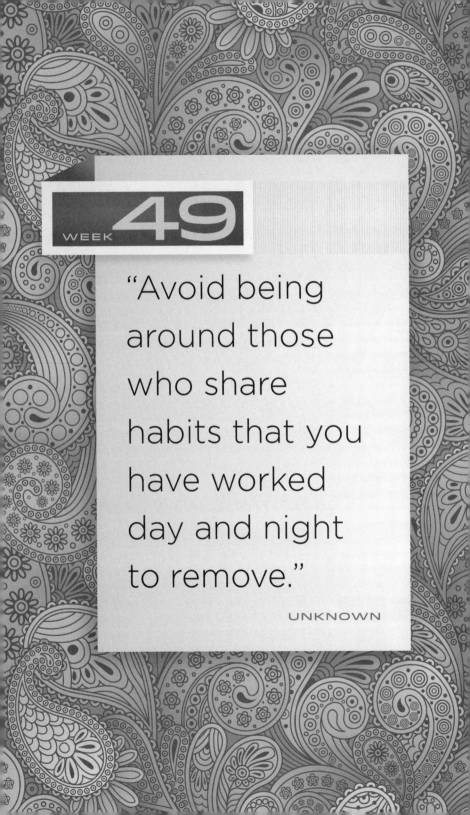

WEEK **49**

"Avoid being around those who share habits that you have worked day and night to remove."

UNKNOWN

MONDAY

Think of the men and women closest to you. How do they influence your actions and decisions?

TUESDAY

What habits are you trying desperately to remove from your life? What are you doing to remove them?

WEDNESDAY

How have you made progress toward weaning bad habits, addictions and unhealthy behavior from your life?

THURSDAY

When have you had success changing an undesirable behavior into a desirable one? Describe what you did to bring about the change.

FRIDAY

What boundaries will you set to keep others from negatively influencing you? What relationships might you need to dissolve for your own health and wellness?

WEEK **50**

"God doesn't
waste anything.
You are not
defined by your
past. You are
prepared by it."

UNKNOWN

MONDAY

Describe a time when something in your like prompted you to ask "why". What happened? What was the outcome?

TUESDAY

Don't waste your pain by failing to learn from it. What lessons have you learned from experiencing pain?

WEDNESDAY

What parts of your past are important to take with you into your future? What parts of your past do you need to bury?

THURSDAY

What challenges do you face right now that could be preparing you for something good in the future?

FRIDAY

When tragedy strikes, how can you change the question from "why me" to "how can I use this"? How would that change your perspective on conflict and trials?

WEEK 51

"Commitment means staying loyal to what you said you were going to do long after the feeling has left you."

UNKNOWN

MONDAY

How seriously do you take the commitments you have made? What factors shape how you feel about the commitments you make?

TUESDAY

What circumstances might cause you to go back on your word, especially when you have made a large commitment?

WEDNESDAY

How can you resist the urge to commit to something, when that commitment is based only on emotions? Why is this so difficult for most of us?

THURSDAY

Which of your current commitments match your life values? Which of your commitments are out of sync with your values?

FRIDAY

Describe the driving force in your life that allows you to maintain commitment and integrity even when you don't feel like it.

WEEK **52**

"Cutting people
out of my life
does not mean
I hate them;
it simply means
I love and
respect me."

UNKNOWN

MONDAY

How can you remove someone from your life out of love instead of out of anger or unforgiveness?

TUESDAY

How can you change the way you interact with the people whom you cannot remove from your life?

WEDNESDAY

What would it mean to respect yourself enough to let someone go from your life?

THURSDAY

What kind of grief process might you have to experience when you remove negative people from your life? How can you work through that process?

FRIDAY

How might removing certain people, attitudes and behaviors from your life free you to live more fully? Name the top three things you know you need to remove from your life. How will you go about removing them?

NOTES

NOTES

ACKNOWLEDGMENTS

First of all, I want to acknowledge my lord and savior, Jesus Christ, for the second chance He's given me to make an impact on this world.

I also would like to thank several others for their important part in this adventure. Thanks go to:

- My father and mother, for introducing me to God at an early age. I have never received a better gift.

- My beautiful wife, Alicia, for all your amazing support. You believed in me even when I did not believe in myself. We have known each other since we were twelve years old, attending Harriett Tubman Middle School together in the sixth grade. I could never repay you or even fully express what you have added to my life as my wife, best friend, business partner, and biggest fan. I would not be the man I am today without your love and support!

- My sons, DaLontae and EJ Broussard, who have taught me a great deal and who have influenced me in ways I can't even describe. Both of you have helped me to become a better father and man.

- My aunt, Audrey M. Broussard-Holmes. As I started this journey more than four years ago, you helped turn my thoughts and ideas into action plans that I have been blessed to share with the world. None of this would have been possible without your love and support from the very beginning.

- My friend, Jessica Lynn Taylor, Ph.D., for your love and support over the last two years, and for your help with this project. It truly would not be what it is without your input. You have helped me process so much and your invaluable assistance is greatly appreciated.

- My friend, workout partner, editor and writer, Steve Halliday, Ph.D. Your friendship and support over the past two years, your guidance and willingness to help me at my pace throughout this process, has made all the difference in the world. You have truly been a Godsend to both my family and to me.

ABOUT THE AUTHOR

Transformation—in a nutshell, that's the core message of **Eldridge J. Broussard III**, one of today's most in-demand speakers.

His own transformation took him on a journey from being a ward of the State of Oregon's foster care system, to its juvenile justice system, and to the Oregon State Correctional System, ultimately to becoming a respected community leader and business professional, sought out for his potent public presentations.

Today, El is passionate about spreading his message of personal transformation. He especially challenges you to *"Own Who You Are"* while deeply exploring your relationships, starting with the most important one, the relationship with yourself. El's compelling insights empower business professionals and corporate clients to reach new levels of success, while equipping and inspiring individuals to make positive and lasting life changes.

El and his beautiful wife, Alicia, live in Portland, Oregon, with their two sons, DaLontae and EJ.

I invite you to contact me with comments about this resource, or to inquire about possible speaking opportunities, at:

www.elspeaks.com.

You can also stay connected with me at the following:

www.facebook.com/elspeaks

www.twitter.com/el_speaks

www.instagram.com/el_speaks